REGULAR SHOW™

GAME NIGHT! QUIPS' BOOK OF QUESTIONS, QUIZZES & GAMES

PSSI
Price Stern Sloan
An Imprint of Penguin Group (USA) LLC

Written by Quips (with lots of help from Brandon T. Snider)

PRICE STERN SLOAN
Published by the Penguin Group
Penguin Group (USA) LLC, 375 Hudson Street, New York, New York 10014, USA

USA | Canada | UK | Ireland | Australia | New Zealand | India | South Africa | China

penguin.com
A Penguin Random House Company

Published in 2014 by Price Stern Sloan, a division of Penguin Young Readers Group, 345 Hudson Street, New York, New York 10014. PSS! is a registered trademark of Penguin Group (USA) LLC. Printed in the USA.

ISBN 978-0-8431-8248-4   10 9 8 7 6 5 4 3 2

TABLE OF CONTENTS

My name is Quips. My cousin is Skips, actually. Funny story . . . I got my name because I'm quippy. Good thing I'm not sappy, or my name would be Saps. Get it? SAPS. Anyway, I took a little break from the com biz (that's short for comedy business), but you can't keep a good jokester down, am I right? ZINGO! So you guys like laughing? Awesome. Say it with me . . .

Who's ready for some FUNNY?!

ZINGO!

RIGBY RULES!

1 **TRUE OR FALSE:**
Rigby once changed his name to Garbage Barge.

2 **Rigby's wrestling doll is named . . . ?**
A) Beef Burrito
B) Bulk Blogan
C) Bald-Spot Terry
D) Prince

3 **How old is Rigby?**
A) 22
B) 23
C) 7
D) Timeless

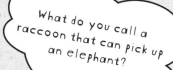

What do you call a raccoon that can pick up an elephant?

Rigby is a raccoon. Pretty wild, right?

4 **TRUE OR FALSE:**
One time, Rigby had surgery that left him looking like he only had ONE butt cheek.

5 **BARRACUDA DEATHWISH is one of Rigby's favorite bands. Who are the three band members?**
A) Sage, Rosemary, and Thyme
B) Salty Steve, Axl, and Ragnarok
C) Crash, Hob Daniels, and The Urge
D) Larry, Daryl, and Daryl

6 **TRUE OR FALSE:**
Rigby is allergic to peanuts.

7 **Rigby is a master at hamboning. What is hamboning?**
A) The art of eating an entire ham in one sitting
B) The ability to make a sandwich in less than a minute
C) The rhythmic slapping of a person's hands against his or her body
D) The reason for the season

You call him SIR! Ha-ha! Get it? Because he's probably huge! And you call huge people SIR! Oh man, this is fun.

What do you call cheese that's not yours?

8 **What is the name of Rigby's favorite place to get grilled cheese sandwiches?**
A) Cheese-o-Rama's
B) Cheesa-Lama-Ding-Dong's
C) Karen Cheddar's House of Cheese & Things
D) Cheezer's

9 **TRUE OR FALSE:**
A Halloween wizard once turned Rigby into a boat.

10 **Rigby has masklophobia, which is the fear of what?**
A) Masks and costumed characters
B) Masklos
C) Tiny men from the 1980s who wear masks and live in a mountain
D) Trick question—Rigby fears nothing!

Nacho cheese! Like it's NOT YOURS! It's slang. ZINGO!

MORDECAI COOL-DE-CAI

1 **Mordecai accidentally unleashed the Guardian of Secrets from which of these places?**
A) The Well of Lies
B) Secretville
C) Margaret's Diary
D) His butt

> Mordecai loves the ladies, huh? Next time he's looking for love, he should use one of my famous lines . . .

2 **TRUE OR FALSE:**
Mordecai tried to join a group of men with blond hair but was kicked out when they discovered he was just wearing a wig.

3 **Mordecai used a website called Couple Corral to score dates with ladies. Which of these ladies did Mordecai NOT find online?**
A) Cloudy Jane aka CJ
B) Flamingo Woman
C) Sally Cries-a-Lot
D) Canary Girl

4 **Rigby forced Mordecai to watch which of these movies?**

A) *Vampire Grandma*
B) *Planet Chasers: Starlight Excellent*
C) *Battle of the Sporks*
D) *Phantom Crumbs and the Cupcake to Nowhere*

5 **TRUE OR FALSE:**

Mordecai went to cooking school, but never finished.

6 **What is the name of the cologne Mordecai wore that attracted a bunch of unicorn bros?**

A) Loner
B) Bakkar Noir
C) Dude Time
D) One Horn

"Hey, girl. Are you from heaven? Because I can see your angel wings . . ."

7 **TRUE OR FALSE:**
Mordecai's favorite band is Burrito Bill and the Hot Sauces.

8 **Which of these is NOT one of Mordecai's nicknames?**
A) Mordecry
B) Brodecai
C) Wrongdecai
D) Coolio St. Awesome

9 **TRUE OR FALSE:**
Mordecai has had braces.

10 **Mordecai has a very special milk shake known by what name?**
A) Mordemilk shake
B) Sandy
C) Mordeshake
D) The Mississippi Queen

Get it? Because girls are like angels! Aw, man, I am GOOD!

1 Mordecai and Rigby taught Gregg the Caveman about language, technology, health and hygiene, laws, music, and everything else. But they forgot one thing. What was it?

A) Love
B) The Robot
C) How to make the perfect olive tapenade
D) Branding

You know, friendship is like a dance . . .

2 **TRUE OR FALSE:**
Mordecai and Rigby once gave Skips a coupon for his birthday that said they would do his chores for one day and one day only.

3 Sometimes when Mordecai and Rigby argue they call each other "turds." Pops stopped them from doing this by offering what solution?

A) Telling them it's very rude to call someone that
B) Telling them that we can all be turds
C) Handing them "hush money"
D) He line-danced until they stopped.

MORDECAI & RIGBY: BEST FRIENDS FOREVER

4 **Mordecai, Rigby, Skips, and Benson have a bowling team. What is the name of their team?**

A) The Park Strikers
B) Pizza, Inc.
C) Mordecai & The Rigbys
D) Jennifer

5 **Mordecai and Rigby are also known as . . .**

A) Mord & Igby
B) Mordo & Rigs
C) Cai & By
D) Dr. Ticklesworth & Professor Fuzzles

It takes TWO to TANGO! Can I get a what what? ZINGO!

6 **Mordecai and Rigby sometimes do solids for each other. What is a solid?**

A) The ability to stop time and give someone a bathroom break
B) An ancient Chinese pizza bagel
C) A quick burst of superpowers
D) A favor

7 **TRUE OR FALSE:**
Rigby accidentally started a Zombocalypse when he smiled at the wrong zombie.

8 **Mordecai and Rigby were arrested and brought before a galactic court for what reason?**
A) They committed crimes against fashion.
B) No reason: The galactic court was just bored.
C) They were deemed "too cool."
D) So they could compete in a dance competition

9 **TRUE OR FALSE:**
Rigby's body once rejected Rigby's consciousness because he was eating too much junk food.

10 **Which of these games do Mordecai and Rigby love to play?**
A) Hide the mountain
B) Patty-cake
C) Rock-paper-scissors
D) Mordecai and Rigby don't have time for games!

I love rock-paper-scissors! I guess I'm just a CUTUP! Get it? Because scissors are used to cut. CLASSIC!

Here's one I've been working on for a while . . .

What did the judge say when the skunk walked into the courtroom?

Wait for it . . .

Odor in the court!

Isn't that good? ODOR IN THE COURT! Because he smells AND he's in court! That is a ZINGO if ever there was one.

COMEDY CORNER

You know why this game is called Drawsome? Because you draw and it's . . . AWESOME! Ha-ha, get it? Man, that is some clever stuff. Anyway, here's how you play:

1 Call your friends and tell them to come over because it's DRAWSOME TIME!

2 Take a small piece of paper and write down a noun. This could be a person, a place, or a thing. That's what the word *noun* means. Zingo!

3 Fold it up and don't show it to anyone.

4 Are your friends there yet? Why don't you check and see . . .

5 Are your friends there NOW? They better be, because you need them!

6 Have a friend time you for thirty seconds while you begin drawing what you wrote on the piece of paper during step #2. You can draw on the opposite page.

7 Your friends have to guess what you're drawing, so make sure you draw really awesomely . . . or **drawesomely**! Get it?

Zingo!

DRAWSOME BREAK!

Draw here!

SKIPS: COUSIN 4 LIFE

1 **TRUE OR FALSE:**
Skips is a rare albino gorilla.

2 **Skips uses which mystical weapon to defeat the evil Klorgbane?**
A) The Harpoon of Harm
B) A suit of armor he bought on sale at Mystical Weapons & Co.
C) The Fists of Justice
D) His mind!

3 **What was Skips's name before he was Skips?**
A) Walks
B) Shimmy
C) Runs
D) Francis

Family is so important, am I right? My cousin Skips is the best. He's so wise. I guess you could call him a SMARTY-PANTS!

4 **TRUE OR FALSE:**
Skips was given eternal youth by the Council of Trendy Youths

5 Every year on his birthday, Skips must perform a ritual in order to remain immortal. What is the name of this ritual?

A) The Worm
B) The Lindy Hop
C) The Spirit Dance
D) Johnny Two-Step's Eight Simple Moves to Ensure Maximum Immortality

6 After mysteriously losing the love of his life, Skips vowed to never stop doing which of these things?

A) Living life to the fullest
B) Working at the Park
C) Showing y'all haters how we do!
D) Skipping

Right? Because he's smart and wears pants! I'm still working on that joke. I'll give it half a ZINGO. ZING!

7 TRUE OR FALSE:
Skips has worked in the Park for over one hundred years.

8 Skips can play which of these instruments?
A) The drums
B) The recorder
C) The butt horn
D) The electric bass guitar

9 TRUE OR FALSE:
Skips combs over his hair to cover his bald spot.

10 Who is this?

A) Techmo
B) Roboticus
C) Kenny, the Park's IT guy
D) Future Skips

Check out this guy! I wonder if he NEEDS A HAND! Uh-oh. I think he's got his EYE ON ME! Zuh-Zuh-ZAMMO!

THE BEST NIGHT OF MY (QUIPS'S) LIFE

My cousin Skips is so cool that he invited me over to play Drawsome with all of his buddies, and it was THE BEST NIGHT OF MY LIFE. Those guys were great! Rigby and Mordecai loved my jokes. I think they might actually be IN LOVE with me. That's how funny I am. People love me! What can I say except . . . ZINGO!

1 **What did Gary bring over when everyone played Drawsome?**

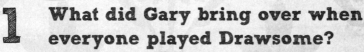

A) Seven-layer dip
B) Taco salad
C) A single onion
D) A positive attitude

2 **Reginald, the giant baby Guardian of the Eternal Youth, majored in which field of study in college?**

A) Partying
B) Kickboxing
C) Communications
D) Omniscience

3 **TRUE OR FALSE:**
Drawsome is supposed to be a safe space that is free of judgment.

4 **What's my (Quips's) last name?**
A) Quippenger
B) Quipplestein
C) Quippendorfer
D) Harrison

5 **TRUE OR FALSE:**

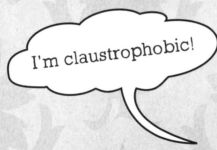

I'm claustrophobic!

6 **What is my (Quips's) most famous catchphrase?**
A) Zabco!
B) Zeemo!
C) Zlacko!
D) Zingo!

These questions are hard, right? It's like math! Hey, what did the math book say to the other math book? Boy, do I have PROBLEMS! Isn't that great? PROBLEMS! Because it's a math book.

7 **TRUE OR FALSE:**
Reginald trapped me (Quips) inside a crystal ball because he didn't like my attitude.

8 **My (Quips's) cousin Skips made me promise not to tell any more jokes, so I decided to become which of these things instead?**

A) Angry

B) A teacher

C) I needed to become more than a man, I needed to become a symbol.

D) A clown

Z to the I to the N to the G to the O! What's that spell? ZINGO!

HOW TO TELL JOKES: A STEP-BY-STEP GUIDE TO BEING HILARIOUS

With my four easy steps to being hilarious, you'll have your friends laughing hysterically in no time at all!

Step 1 Be hilarious.

Step 2 Write some funny jokes.

Step 3 Hit 'em with the HA-HA!

Step 4 Watch the laughter start rollin' in . . .

See? It's just **THAT EASY!** Use this space to create YOUR jokes. Write down whatever you want! Soon you'll be making crowds laugh from here to the Catskills!

YOUR JOKES HERE

THE BENSON-A-TOR

1 **What is the name of the person who once replaced Benson as park manager?**
A) Darthon
B) Ybgir
C) Ace Balthazar
D) Susan

2 **TRUE OR FALSE:**
Benson has a mug that says: "Canada's Greatest Man."

3 **Benson is a skilled stick-hockey player. What is his stick-hockey code name?**
A) The Benson-a-tor
B) Death Dragon
C) Stick-Hockey Hannigan
D) Captain Gumball

Do you guys like food? Food is great, isn't it? I eat it all the time. Hey, can you guess why the tomato turned red? It saw the salad dressing! ZINGO!

4 Which of these combinations is NOT part of the disgusting drink called The Mississippi Queen?

A) Calamari, ketchup, and salt
B) Kimchi, clam shells, and mayo
C) Pasta sauce, sashimi, and chili peppers
D) Shrimp, chuco, and soy sauce

5 TRUE OR FALSE:
Benson had a girlfriend named Cindy who left him for Pops.

6 Which of these is NOT in Benson's House Rules book?

A) No harpsichord playing after 10:00 p.m.
B) No unicorns
C) No one named Chauncey is allowed on the grounds at any time.
D) No food on the floor

7 TRUE OR FALSE:
Benson is left-handed.

So many awesome fruits and vegetables out there! Can't forget my grapes, right? Love those grapes. Hey, what did the grape do when it got stepped on? Oh man, you guys are going to freak when you hear the answer . . .

8 **Benson used to play the drums for which famous hair-metal band?**
A) Phoenix & The Ashes
B) Hair to the Throne
C) Coiff
D) Knights of Carnage

9 **TRUE OR FALSE:**
Benson does NOT actually live in the Park.

10 **Who is this?**

A) Snackles the Talking Vending Machine
B) Bruce Snackenheimer, Automat Assassin
C) Benson's adopted brother, Rob
D) Gene, the park manager at East Pines

It let out a little wine!
ZINGO, ZANGO, ZINGO!

POP GOES THE POPS

1 **What is the name of Pops's creepy doll?**

A) Percy

B) Madison St. Cloud

C) Venture

D) Magnolia

You guys ever open a door? It's so easy, right? It's like ... knock, knock! Hey, do you guys like knock-knock jokes? I'll start.

2 **Which of these items does Pops own?**

A) The world's smallest table

B) A harpsichord

C) A secret jungle hideout

D) A coat made **for** kittens **by** kittens

3 **TRUE OR FALSE:**

Pops's last name is a secret only three people in the world know.

KNOCK, KNOCK!

Then you say, "Who's there?"

4 **Pops has a subscription to which of these magazines?**
A) *Candy Trends Weekly*
B) *Fancy Baby*
C) *Tiny Top Hat Quarterly*
D) *Mustaches Monthly*

5 **TRUE OR FALSE:**
Pops owns a car that he calls Carmenita.

6 **In the realm of Darthon, Pops took on which of the following personas?**
A) Señor Gaseosa
B) Lord Headington III
C) Pops ULTRA
D) Cyborg Cowboy

Then you say, "Boo who?"

7 **Where is Pops from?**
A) Lolliland
B) Candy Country
C) Cincinnati
D) The Land of Dreams

8 **Pops keeps which of these things in a barn?**
A) Two very angry cows
B) His secret daughter, Amanda
C) A yellow taxicab
D) An even smaller barn

9 **TRUE OR FALSE:**
Pops can often be seen running around the Park naked.

10 **Pops plays the keyboard in which of these songs?**
A) "Gimme All That Pizza!"
B) "Love Is a Mini Mart"
C) "A Wind Named Barbara"
D) "Aw, Snap!"

Aw, don't cry! It's just a joke!

MUSCLE MAN & FRIENDS

Muscle Man is like that dinosaur that never took a bath . . . the Stinkosaurus! ZINGO!

1 **What is Muscle Man's real name?**
A) Klorgbane
B) Mitch Sorenstein
C) Musculus Mannington
D) Barry

2 **TRUE OR FALSE:**
Muscle Man has never been inside a fancy restaurant.

3 **Muscle Man was on the cover of which of these magazines?**
A) *Video Game Monthly*
B) *Gut*
C) *Modern Woodworking*
D) *Dark Companion Quarterly*

4 **TRUE OR FALSE:**
Muscle Man was pranked by Mordecai and Rigby into believing that he was chosen to be the face of a monster-makeup company.

5 Muscle Man famously makes jokes about which of his family members?
A) His dad
B) His cousin, Karl
C) His mom
D) Muscle Man doesn't joke.

6 What's the name of Hi Five Ghost's brother?
A) Kevin
B) Down Low Ghost
C) Low Five Ghost
D) D'Casper

Ever wonder why ghosts are such bad liars?

7 Which of these is NOT one of Hi Five Ghost's nicknames?

A) H. Fiver G-Unit
B) Fives
C) HFG
D) High Five

8 Where does Muscle Woman work?

A) At an ice-cream shop
B) Icy Hot Jewelry & Apparel
C) Skirt Warehouse
D) Muscle Woman doesn't work because she's independently wealthy.

36

9 **TRUE OR FALSE:** Muscle Woman once broke up with Muscle Man because she thought he smelled like a barnyard.

10 **What is Muscle Woman's real name?**
   A) Ivana Fartalot
   B) Rose
   C) Frunda Gliebkin
   D) Starla Gutsmandottir

ZINGO!

ZAMMO! ZINGO!

I'm on a roll! You can't stop me!

WHO SAID IT?!

1 "You can't touch music, but music can touch you."

2 "I know everything, remember?"

3 "I never realized that accounting can be so fascinating!"

4 "Never pass out when there are markers about!"

5 "GUYS NIGHT!!"

6 "There's no way you got a bingo that fast."

7 "Hey, guys. Here's your coffee."

"Life is like a box of chocolates . . . it can be really sweet but also messy."

39

8 "Hold it. You're not on the list."

9 "Hey, so, thanks for saving all our lives and stuff. That was really brave of you."

10 "It's all right! I'm rich—I can buy another limo!"

That's really smart, right? I should put that on a T-shirt!

COMEDY CORNER 2: THE FUNNY RETURNS

You guys like impressions? I bet you do.

Here's my impression of a hot dog . . . .

Arf, sizzle! Arf, sizzle!

Get it? Because a dog says **arf** and a hot dog sizzles on the grill!

ZINGO!

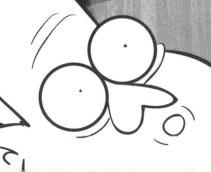

HELLO, LADIES!

1 **Margaret and Eileen work at which of these places?**
A) The Coffee Shop
B) The Café
C) The Restaurant
D) Taco Tim's Salsa Emporium

2 **TRUE OR FALSE:**
Rigby once threw a package of hot dogs at Eileen.

3 **Margaret and Mordecai were trapped in the Friend Zone because . . . ?**
A) It takes two to make a thing go right.
B) They couldn't agree on where to eat dinner.
C) Mordecai waited too long to give Margaret a kiss.
D) Rigby exiled them there out of jealousy.

4 **TRUE OR FALSE:**
Margaret is horrible at baking pies.

5 **Mordecai, Rigby, Margaret, and
Eileen were once attacked by which
of these forest creatures?**
A) Marsh Dude
B) Stag-Man
C) Jean, the Very Bossy Sparrow
D) Ms. Tree

6 **TRUE OR FALSE:**
Eileen is allergic to "horse wind."

These ladies love to dance. Do you know how you make a tissue dance?

7 What is Margaret's last name?

A) Margaretson
B) Bodnar
C) Quetzalcoatl
D) Smith

8 Mordecai and Margaret have been to which of these locations?

A) Kissyface Point
B) Cuddle Cul-De-Sac
C) Snug Harbor
D) Make-Out Mountain

You put a little boogie in it!

ZINGO!

WILD CARDS

1 **Which of these powers does Eagle Man NOT have?**
A) Sonic Shield
B) Power Sword
C) Rocket Fist
D) Butt Blast

2 **RGB2 appeared in which famous television sitcom?**
A) *Hello, There!*
B) *That's My Television*
C) *RGB2 & You*
D) *Turn That Thing OFF!*

How did the barber win the race? He knew a shortcut!

3 **TRUE OR FALSE:**
Thomas the Goat works as an intern in the Park on occasion.

ZINGO!

4 Rigby's brother, Don, loves to give everyone a special kind of hug that he calls what?

A) Sugar

B) Strick-9

C) Don-er-cise

D) Tickle Timez

5 **TRUE OR FALSE:**

Peeps is a giant baby chicken whom Rigby nursed back to health.

6 Gary, Death, the Wizard, and one of the Guardians of Eternal Youth have a bowling team. What is the name of their team?

A) The Joe Blows
B) Gary & Friends
C) Eternal Friendship
D) The Magical Elements

7 Garret Bobby Ferguson was the universal record holder for which video game?

A) *Lemon Chef*
B) *Deli Dude*
C) *Strong Johns*
D) *Broken Bonez*

8 TRUE OR FALSE:
Jeremy the Ostrich is the guy Margaret left so she could be with Mordecai.

Wait for it . . . .

9 What is the name of Gregg the Caveman's girlfriend?

A) T'Keisha
B) Gruella
C) Diane
D) Candace

10 Who are these two?

A) Trash & Scabitha
B) Deborah Debris & Sore Sally
C) The Dropout Twins
D) Trouble

ON A DIET! Because he's five hundred pounds! He totally needs to go on a diet, right? Oh man, that is a big cow! ZINGO!

DEATH KWON DO

1 **Rigby and Mordecai got into an argument over which video game?**
A) *Dig Champs*
B) *Dig Buddies*
C) *Dig Amigos*
D) *Dig or Be Dug*

2 **TRUE OR FALSE:**
Mordecai and Rigby tried to settle their dispute by playing Punchies.

What do you call a pig that knows karate?

3 **Which of these techniques is NOT featured in the book _Death Kwon Do_?**
A) Bicep Flex of Death
B) Pelvic Thrust of Death
C) The Death Saunter
D) The Death Dump

4 **TRUE OR FALSE:**
The Sensai owns a restaurant called Death Kwon Do Pizza Kitchen.

WHO ARE YOU?!

1 Which of the following best describes your personality?

A) I play by my own rules!
B) I'm always cleaning up my friends' messes.
C) Tense? Of course I'm tense!
D) Live and let live, brother.
E) I'm sweet like a candy cane.
F) I don't know. Why don't you ask MY MOM!

2 What kinds of movies do you like?

A) Action!
B) Comedy
C) Who has time for movies?
D) I'm partial to documentaries.
E) Ooooo, I like animation!
F) Anything about MY MOM!

Wow. These questions are heavy. Time to get serious ...

3 If you could throw a party anywhere on Earth, where would you throw it?

A) Aw, man. We have to throw a party on Earth? What about space?!?
B) The arcade would be a cool place.
C) Don't even think about throwing a party in the Park!
D) Someplace nice and simple.
E) Oh my! I love parties! But my arms are weak, and it's hard for me to throw.
F) MY MOM's house!

4 How do you generally start your day?

A) Wake up. Get into trouble.
B) Wake up. Help my friend get out of trouble.
C) Wake up? I barely went to sleep!
D) Wake up. Take things as they come.
E) Wake up. Whisper a secret in my doll's ear. Prance!
F) Wake up. Eat breakfast. Call MY MOM.

5 If there was a movie of your life, what would it be called?

A) *Wild Man and the Magic Taco*
B) *Welcome to Chilltown*
C) *Get Off of My Lawn 2*
D) *The Mariner's Quest*
E) *Sweet Treat Goes to Cupcake Town*
F) *Return of MY MOM*

6 Which of these skills do you possess?

A) The ability to get away with anything!
B) Trustworthiness
C) Patience (but not a lot of it)
D) Peace of mind
E) A positive attitude
F) MY MOM says I'm lazy.

Just kidding! ZINGO! I totally had you fooled! DOUBLE ZINGO!

7 **When you are faced with an unfamiliar problem, what do you usually do?**

A) Run away and get help!
B) Try not to run away.
C) Yell!
D) Solve it.
E) I'm scared just thinking about it!
F) Ask MY MOM what to do.

8 **When you are playing a game, how important is it for you to win?**

A) I love to win! Winning is awesome!
B) Winning is cool.
C) Winning is the only thing!
D) Winning isn't everything.
E) I'm just happy to play a game!
F) If I won something I'd give it to MY MOM.

I wish I knew who I was . . .

YOU ARE . . .

If you answered A to most of the questions, you are RIGBY!

You're a fly-by-the-seat-of-your-pants kind of person who loves adventure, even though it often gets you into trouble.

If you answered B to most of the questions, you are MORDECAI!

You love to chill out and relax. Your friends are really important to you, and they look to you for guidance and support.

If you answered C to most of the questions, you are BENSON!

You're focused and driven. Sometimes too much! It wouldn't hurt you to loosen up a little.

If you answered D to most of the questions, you are SKIPS!

You're peaceful and calm. You try not to let other people's drama affect you, but when it does you're always there to help.

If you answered E to most of the questions, you are POPS!

You live in a magical dreamworld filled with candy, happiness, and little baby bunnies hopping on your belly.

If you answered F to most of the questions, you are MUSCLE MAN!

You're a weirdo who is obsessed with your own mother. You should seek professional help before it's too late.

RIGBY RULES! ANSWERS

1. False: He changed his name to Trash Boat.
2. A. Beef Burrito
3. B. 23
4. True
5. C. Crash, Hob Daniels, and The Urge
6. False: He's allergic to eggs.
7. C. The rhythmic slapping of a person's hands against his or her body.
8. D. Cheezer's
9. False: He was actually turned into a house.
10. A. Masks and costumed characters

Time to tally everything up! Let's see that score, smarty-pants!

MORDECAI, COOL-DE-CAI ANSWERS

1. C. Margaret's Diary
2. True
3. A. Cloudy Jane aka CJ
4. B. *Planet Chasers: Starlight Excellent*
5. False: He went to art school and never finished.
6. C. Dude Time
7. False: His favorite band is Brain Explosion.
8. D. Coolio St. Awesome
9. True
10. C. Mordeshake

MORDECAI & RIGBY: BEST FRIENDS FOREVER ANSWERS

1. A. Love
2. True
3. B. Telling them that we can all be turds.
4. A. The Park Strikers
5. B. Mordo & Rigs
6. D. A favor
7. False: It was when he accidentally put a tape in a 3-D movie projector backward.
8. C. They were deemed "too cool."
9. True
10. C. Rock-paper-scissors

SKIPS: COUSIN 4 LIFE ANSWERS

1   False: He's actually a yeti.
2   C. The Fists of Justice
3   A. Walks
4   False: Skips was given eternal youth by the Guardians of Eternal Youth.
5   C. The Spirit Dance
6   D. Skipping
7   True
8   D. The electric bass guitar
9   True
10 A. Techmo

Do smarties even WEAR pants? Am I right? ZINGO!

THE BEST NIGHT OF MY (QUIPS'S) LIFE ANSWERS

1   A. Seven-layer dip
2   C. Communications
3   True
4   A. Quippenger
5   True
6   D. Zingo!
7   False: He trapped me (Quips) inside a cube because he didn't like my jokes.
8   D. A clown

THE BENSON-A-TOR ANSWERS

1   D. Susan
2   False: It says "World's Greatest Boss."
3   B. Death Dragon
4   A. Calamari, ketchup, and salt
5   False: He once had a girlfriend named Veronica who left him for a "businessman."
6   C. No one named Chauncey is allowed on the grounds at any time.
7   True
8   B. Hair to the Throne
9   True: He lives in an apartment near the Park.
10 D. Gene, the park manager at East Pines

POP GOES THE POPS ANSWERS

1 A. Percy
2 B. A harpsichord
3 False: His last name is Maellard.
4 D. *Mustaches Monthly*
5 True
6 D. Cyborg Cowboy
7 A. Lolliland
8 C. A yellow taxicab
9 True
10 D. "Aw, Snap!"

Almost there! Hey, did you hear about that big cat that ran really fast?

MUSCLE MAN & FRIENDS ANSWERS

1 B. Mitch Sorenstein
2 False: He took Muscle Woman's parents to a fancy restaurant in order to impress them!
3 A. *Video Game Monthly*
4 False: He was actually pranked into believing he won the lottery.
5 C. His mom
6 C. Low Five Ghost
7 A. H. Fiver G-Unit
8 B. Icy Hot Jewelry & Apparel
9 False: It was because he didn't show his feelings.
10 D. Starla Gutsmandottir

WHO SAID IT? ANSWERS

1 Mordecai
2 Skips
3 Pops
4 Rigby
5 Hi Five Ghost
6 Benson
7 Eileen
8 Bobby
9 Margaret
10 Mr. Maellard

He was a CHEETAH! Ha-ha! I love that one. What I'm saying is that you shouldn't cheat. It's totally not cool. Stay in school, too!

HELLO, LADIES! ANSWERS

1   A. The Coffee Shop
2   True
3   C. Mordecai waited too long to give Margaret a kiss.
4   True: After a pie contest, Mordecai once told Margaret her pie was "burned and raw" and that it "tasted like barf!"
5   B. Stag-Man
6   False: She's allergic to duck dander.
7   D. Smith
8   D. Make-Out Mountain

WILD CARDS ANSWERS

1   D. Butt Blast
2   B. *That's My Television*
3   True
4   A. Sugar
5   False: Peeps is a giant floating eyeball that sees everything we do.
6   D. The Magical Elements
7   D. *Broken Bonez*
8   False: Jeremy was hired by Benson to be Mordecai's replacement, but he turned down the job.
9   C. Diane
10 A. Trash & Scabitha

DEATH KWON DO ANSWERS

1   A. *Dig Champs*
2   True
3   C. The Death Saunter
4   False: It's actually called Death Kwon Do Pizza and Subs

FINAL SCORE

100+ Points
You are a

TECHNOMANCER!

80+ Points
You are a

WARRIOR KNIGHT!

70+ Points
You are a

PIRATE SAMURAI!

60+ Points
You are a

VAMPIRE-ARCHER!

50+ Points
You are a

CYBORG COWBOY!

Fewer than 50 Points ...
Time to watch more *Regular Show!* Yeah-yuh!